Astromasks
Astrology Decoded

Published and Distributed by:

Cosmic Attractions Research and Consultancy
1301 Oakdale Road # 22
Modesto, CA 95355
U.S.A.

Astromasks

A speculative theory and research in astrology

"In the past, many without much conviction have reported on astrology and its connections to human physiognomy. In this book, the author introduces a new theory of complementary pairs to give new meanings to the zodiac signs, and also to explain their relationship to human physiognomy, for the very first time in the history of astrology."

Astromasks

Astrology Decoded

Vijay Rishii Ph.D.

☼ Contents ☼

Dedications

Astrology is the only universal religion, and Linda Goodman, the Goddess of Astrology, who dedicated her entire life searching for the truth and spread her wisdom to millions throughout the world. Thank you Linda, for teaching me this spiritual science, which has moulded my soul into the person I am today. And, for inspiring me to follow up my hobby of trying to recognize the sun signs of people into a deeper observation, which resulted in the compilation of this book, dedicated to you. Being one among the millions of fans who missed the chance of ever meeting you in person, yet we know you and feel you through every single word written in your books, from where I have borrowed some of your wisdom and ideas.

To my dear dad, A. Rajendran, with his tender virgoen heart, is only one of the very few in the class of late virgoen, Mother Theresa, and to my loving mom, A.R. Lilypushpam, who spreads compassion in her Geminian ways. Thank you for bringing me into this wonderful earth and for all the love, freedom and support, my heartfelt thanks to you. To my late grandfather, E.A.S. Arumugam Nadar, an amateur astrologer, who roughly plotted my life journey, the day I was born. Thank you for passing on the astrological genes and intuitions to me.

To all my brothers, A.R. Malairajan, A.R. Jeyakumar, A.R. Babu, and all my family members for the love and happiness you give me, and for accepting me the way I am, weird, whenever I started my astro-philosophical lectures. To all my friends and others who touched my life in one way or the other, during my four different lives in four different countries. I thank you all.

To my friend, Jeff Pellas, my neighbor friend in State college, Pennsylvania, with an extraordinary talent for drawing and painting, who was one of the main inspirations behind this project. Without his help, this book would have been another one of my procrastinations in life. Thank you, Jeff, for everything.

Last but not least, to my lovely son Rishii and my daughter Meena for all the happiness you give me. I am so lucky to have you both in my life.

Since Linda really wished to be known to the world as a poet, I wish to dedicate two of my following poems to her and to all the true love in this universe.

Linda Goodman

Elements of Love

Ever since I gazed into your soft glowing eyes,
They have cast a deep mystery into my eyes.

Ever since my ears heard your smooth silky voice,
They have remained yearning to hear thy voice.

Every time I take a deep look into my soul,
I can see an invisible bond linking our souls.

Every time a thought of you pops into my mind,
I can recall the sweet memories filled in my mind.

Every time I listen to the beat of my heart,
I can hear the songs of pure love filled in your heart.

Every time my hands touch your soft tender body,
I can feel a strange wave of peace flow over my body.

Feelings...

Feelings, yet another of the many confusing words,
For, they are just like the passing clouds.

Feelings come and go before you hardly see,
For, they are like tides in the sea.

Feelings are waves of mind with no reasons,
For they come in cycles like the seasons.

Feelings sometimes are pure as snow in December,
For they are just dreams you seldom remember.

Feelings change with time and keep coming more,
For if not, they are not feelings anymore.

Feelings, the only life force on earth so far,
For which, the life is worth living for.

Feelings are the bonds that link us all,
For without which, life has no meaning at all.

Feelings with no control could make one blind,
For feelings sure, leave you confused in mind.

Feelings of worry are like a wasted gold,
For life is short on this temporal world.

Feelings of happiness are what we all need,
For which, love is the only universal feeling indeed.

Preface

The beauty and mystery of the night sky have fascinated human since before the dawn of civilization. Though, by and large, the heavens remained mysterious and awesome, earliest writings in cuneiform and hieroglyphics, some 6000 years ago, bear witness to a thorough knowledge of the stars and constellations. Thus, the foundations for Astronomy had been long laid before human understanding of the other sciences. In those days, priest-astronomers observed the rhythms of the heavens to establish calendars and looked to the heavens for signs that would indicate the will of their gods, whom they believed ruled human lives. Their reading and study of the stars led to the pseudoscience of astrology. So, in the beginning and far more than 2000 years, astronomy and astrology were the same science. Astrology - the study of the supposed influence of celestial bodies on human, has been differently interpreted, developed, and used by the various civilizations ever since. The ancient civilizations are gone, but their gift of astrology still survives among us. If astrology were just a superstitious belief, it would long ago have taken its place alongside our ancestors in the footnotes of history. Alone, among the sciences, astrology has spanned the centuries and made the journey intact. We shouldn't be surprised about the fact that it still remains with us, unchanged by time – because astrology is truth and truth is eternal.

Since the discovery by Copernicus that the earth was not the center of the universe but traveled round the sun, the discovery of new planets, and the development of modern astronomy, did not destroy astrology, though it was undermined. Today, though astrology has lost some of its ancient flavors, since the pace of our lives have increased tremendously during the last 100 years; it still remains as a curious subject for many. With practitioners in nearly every country, astrology's popularity is stronger than ever. Almost every magazines and newspapers add astrology in a small column as a vitamin for the readers. Most of such columns are filled with general phrases, but give a pint of positive hope for the readers about what is in store for the week or month ahead. Astrology, as a serious subject, begins with the reading of a person's natal horoscope and the relative positions of the planets at the present time with respect to the natal chart. In this ever-hurrying life of ours, nobody has the time for such theoretical analysis. Most of us take what we get, blame the rest on somebody, and accept a few as god-given punishment.

Beyond the laborious analysis of the horoscope, astrology can be a very important tool in the psychoanalysis of human personality and the behavioral patterns in a given situation. For example, in relationships (which is one of the serious troubles in our society today), in medicine, and also in criminal investigations. The true potentials of astrology are yet to be discovered and exploited, much for the reasons that, astrology lacks physical proof, factual explanations, or any scientific evidence. Recently, tremendous efforts are being made in the astrological community, to prove the validity of astrology in the scientific world by way of research, and also to integrate astrology into the mainstream of social and psychological sciences. But still, astrology remains as an unexplored science, and is not even recognized as a science by many, without a well-defined, strong foundation.

We call ourselves Aries, Gemini, Libra etc., from only the position of the Sun (sun sign) during the time of our birth. Many astrologers believe that a person's 80 percent personality can be seen from the sun sign characteristics alone, which is mostly true since sun has the most powerful influence on everything within our solar system. Sun sign personalities have been thoroughly studied, and illustrated at best, in the astrological best seller, Linda Goodman's Sun signs. In-depth exploration of the complex relationship compatibility between different sun sign personalities of both sexes have been explained with breathtaking accuracy in the all time classical book of Linda Goodman's Love Signs. I am not a professional astrologer, but astrology is my religion and Linda's books are my Bible, Geetha, Koran and everything else to me. I read Linda's first book on sun signs when I was 18 years old and there began my hobby to recognize the sun signs of people. Though most of the time I was wrong, but I was sometimes right in guessing the ascendants. My first level of training went this way. By simple observations of a person's looks and behaviors (introvert, extrovert, noisy etc.), I categorized the person into one of the four elements, fire, earth, air, or water, which I later confirmed it with my subject. The next step was to classify the subject into the type of sun sign, cardinal, fixed or mutable. Once I got these two correct, I got my score. Thanks to my cousin and my alter ego, Shivy, for playing with me this astrological puzzle.

After reading Linda's book on sun signs a hundred times or more during the last 24 years, I came to find that not only did the characters described for each sign were accurate, but also some of the physical features seen on the face for some of the sun sign personalities were very obvious. More than my amazement for the accurate description of the sun sign personalities, I was very much intrigued by the physical features described by Linda. Since then, I started looking for physical evidences on the faces of people, to solve my astrological puzzle of recognizing the sun signs. Here began my study on the relation between sun sign and physical features.

Recognizing the sun signs of people from the physical appearance alone is very obvious only in a few cases, while it is very difficult in general. In order to solve the above mentioned problem, and also to find an explanation for the ascendant characters seen on a person's face, I started looking deeply into the faces of people, searching for clues that would throw some light into my quest. I wish to apologize here to the people who were annoyed by my constant stares. On final analysis, the results of my search led to a new theory in astrology. I have observed sufficient physical evidences on individual's faces to support my theory, which will be the main theme of this book.

Based on my experience in astrology, six vital factors, namely, position of the Sun (sun sign), the Ascendant (earth sign), position of the Moon (moon sign), position of Mercury, position of Mars and position of Venus determine the physiological and psychological make up of an individual. Thus, the first six inner celestial bodies are responsible for the design of our astro-personality, while the outer, larger planets decide our life path and our future generation in the long run. From observations, I came to find that the visible, physical characters are designed only by the three major chart factors, namely, the sun sign, ascendant and moon sign, respectively. The influence of other inner planets on the physical features is not so evident, and therefore, will not be significant in our further discussions. Although, Mercury designs our mind, Venus our heart, and Mars our general drive in life. I would like to call ascendant as "Earth sign", since it's an earth factor that depends on the time, latitude and longitude on earth, where the particular event is occurring. The name, earth sign, will be explained in more detail later in this book.

I am sure there is more to add to this speculative theory and research, which is certainly not complete in many ways. Astrology has been differently interpreted, studied, understood, and accepted by various people. Here, I present to you the way I view astrology, the meanings of the zodiac symbols, and their connections to the facial features seen in human. I have compiled 10 years of my research in western astrology in this book called, **"ASTROMASKS"**, which I hope will throw some new light into this ancient science. I have introduced the theory of complimentary pairs to explain the true meanings behind zodiac signs for the first time in the history of astrology. I have integrated astrology to the evolution of animals on earth, and our genetic connections to these land mammals. I have given physical evidence to support my theory and discussions in this book. Photographs and pictures will be given as actual physical proofs for all my interpretations and explanations. This book is a preliminary study and a first step to show the real connections between the zodiac signs and we human on earth with physical evidences. The main aim of this book, and my humble attempt through this book, is to bring astrology to the limelight and to prove its validity as a science. Although I have only given new meanings to the zodiac signs, the construction of horoscopes, their interpretations, and the chart factors remain the same. Some of you could find my views interesting and thought provoking, while it could be confusing and disturbing for the traditional astrologers and people with a religious conviction. In general, I hope you enjoy this journey with me, to ponder yet another mystery in the learning of this amazing subject, science, and religion of Astrology. Come on! Let's uncover the masks.

Vijay Rishii

History of Astrology

The history of astrology encompasses a great span of human history and many cultures. The recorded history of astrology dates back to 3000-4000 BC, and believed to be born in the land of Mesopotamia, which is geographically in modern Iraq. Apparently, the Babylonians were the first civilization to have mastered this ancient science and extensively used in their national and political affairs. The exact chronology of the birth and development of astrology is still elusive to modern day astrologers throughout the world. Astrology along with its twin-sister astronomy is believed to have originated at the same time in human history. The terms astrology and astronomy have been closely related until recently, when the scientific revolution surged and astronomy gained more respect, while astrology lost some of its original flavors due to the lack of scientific evidence. So, astronomy became a scientific study of celestial objects such as stars, planets, comets, galaxies and phenomena that originate outside the earth's atmosphere. And, astrology became a skeptical, pseudoscience that involves study of the correlations between the positions of various celestial objects and the affairs of human beings and other life on earth.

Today, one can only speculate on the reasons for the birth of this mysterious art or science that the synchronous movement of the celestial bodies relative to the earth had a discernible effect on human life. From the simple reasons for the cycle of four seasons, which are caused by the position of earth relative to the sun, ancient human observed similar effects caused by the position of the planets in our solar system. Thus astrology grew as an experiential science based on observations and recordings. Astrology has played a major role in our society since the beginning of civilizations, and may be even before that. Its influence can be seen in almost every part of the world. After the Babylonians, the Greeks began their immense influence on astrology during 400-500 BC. The Greeks were responsible for incorporating mythology into astrology. The terms used in astrology today like zodiac, horoscope, the names and the mythological figures of the signs of the zodiac are derived from Greek. From Greece astrology spread to Rome, Egypt, India and other Arabic countries. In Central America, the Mayans and the Aztecs developed their own form of astrology. The Chinese developed their own astrology around 300 BC based on twelve animals representing each year, which was then adopted and used in Japan, Thailand, Vietnam and other East Asian countries.

Astrology thrived in Europe during 1300-1600 AD, when renowned astronomers like Galileo Galilei, Tycho Brahe and Johannes Kepler were themselves practicing astrologers. The most famous predictions about European and world affairs were made by the French astrologer Nostradamus, who became famous after the publication of his work *Centuries*, which was a series of prophecies in cryptic verse. His predictions have been interpreted as relating to a great variety of events, including the French and English Revolutions, and the Second World War. William Lilly was a famed English astrologer who caused much controversy for allegedly predicting the Great Fire of London some 14 years before it happened, for which, he was tried for the offence in parliament but later was found to be innocent.

In 1600 AD, Nicolaus Copernicus was the first astronomer to formulate the scientific theory of heliocentric universe, which displaced the earth from the center of the universe. The foundation of astrology was already laid based on the geocentric theory of the universe, which is evident in the way a horoscope is constructed even today. Alan Leo, who is considered the father of modern day astrology, is credited as being one of the most important astrologers in the 20th century because of his stimulating work in the revival of astrology in the west after its general downfall in the 17th century.

In the United States, a great surge of popular interest in astrology took place in the beginning of 1900 AD sparked by a very popular astrologer based in New York City named Evangeline Adams who helped feed the public's thirst for astrology readings with many accurate forecasts. The inspiring works by astrologers such as Alan Leo, Sepharial, Charles Carter, among others, further led to the surge of interest in astrology by wide distribution of astrological journals, text, papers, and textbooks of astrology throughout the United States. The period after the First World War gave way to the popular media influence on the great public interest in astrology. Publishers realized that millions of readers were interested in astrological forecasts and the interest grew ever more intense. Journalists began to write articles based on character descriptions and astrological forecasts were published in newspapers based on the month and day of birth, as taken from the position of the Sun when a person is born. This led to modern-day publishing of Sun Sign astrology columns and expanded further to many astrological books and magazines. Today, there are three main branches of astrology in the world, namely Western astrology, Indian or Jyotish astrology, and Chinese or East Asian astrology. The entire discussions in this book are based on tropical western astrology.

A closer look at the zodiac

When we remain stargazing on a clear moonless night, we can easily recognize the patterns the bright stars make. These patterns of stars, called the constellations, have changed scarcely at all since the time of the first great civilizations some 6000 years ago and will not change perceptibly in our lifetime. Altogether, there are 88 or more recognized constellations, which we know from the records kept by ancient stargazers in the Middle East – in Babylon and Egypt. The Greeks named the constellations after gods, heroes, creatures and objects that featured in their mythology, matching the star patterns to the mythological figures. Though for many constellations one needs an active imagination, in some instances, the constellation patterns really do look like the figures they are intended to represent. Since this book is limited to astrology, we will focus ourselves only to the imaginary band in the heavens, in which the Sun, Moon and other Planets are always found, called the Zodiac. In astrology, the word **Zodiac** is derived from the Greek words, ***zodiakos kyklos*** meaning circle of animals that denotes an annual cycle of twelve constellations along the ecliptic through which the sun and the planets move across the heavens seen from the earth (See Figure 1).

Babylonian astronomers developed the zodiac of twelve signs, which is recognized as the first known celestial coordinate system. The zodiac remains in use in modern tropical astrology where the celestial sphere is divided into twelve equal zones with 30° longitude for each sign. In a June, 2007 article published in **Nature**, titled, *Fathers of the zodiac tracked down*, reported that, "using modern techniques and some rocks US astronomer

Brad Schaefer has traced the origin of a set of ancient clay tablets that display constellations thought to be precursors of the present-day zodiac to 1370 BC". The tablets contain nearly 200 astronomical observations, including measurements related to several constellations. They are written in cuneiform, a Middle-Eastern script that is one of the oldest known forms of writing, and were made in Babylon. When we look at the zodiac signs in the celestial sphere, the sun crosses the equinox at 0° Aries in March 21, which marks the beginning of spring in the northern hemisphere. Aries is the first sign of the zodiac, and the sequence follows till Pieces at 330° as listed below in Table 1.

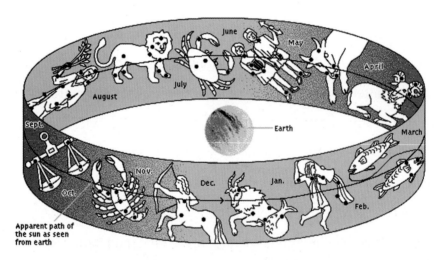

Figure 1

When we look closer at the sequence of the elements starting from Aries, we see that it is Fire – Earth – Air – Water. On scrutiny of this sequence one can decipher the encoded message of the way everything began on planet earth. When one interprets the meaning behind this sequence; at the beginning, the earth was a ball of fire, which on cooling became solidified earth releasing gases that formed the atmosphere or air, and when the air condensed it formed liquid or water. And we all can agree that life began from water, which is evident from the way every animal is born into this world, including us humans in a bag of amniotic fluid. Our Babylonian ancestors could have called Aries as a water sign or Taurus as a fire sign, but instead followed the sequence Fire – Earth – Air – Water, which is definitely not a coincidence to the way everything began on planet earth. And, as we go around the zodiac circle we see that the same sequence is maintained till the last water sign Pisces. Similarly, the sequence Cardinal – Fixed – Mutable, along with trine of elements every 120° is maintained around the entire zodiac circle. Also, the air signs are always opposed by fire signs and the earth signs are always opposed by water signs, and so on.

Astro-Sign	Zodiac Sign	Element	Quality
Aries	The Ram	Fire	Cardinal
Taurus	The Bull	Earth	Fixed
Gemini	The Twins	Air	Mutable
Cancer	The Crab	Water	Cardinal
Leo	The Lion	Fire	Fixed
Virgo	The Virgin	Earth	Mutable
Libra	The Scales	Air	Cardinal
Scorpio	The Scorpion	Water	Fixed
Sagittarius	The Archer	Fire	Mutable
Capricorn	The Goat	Earth	Cardinal
Aquarius	The Water bearer	Air	Fixed
Pisces	The Two Fish	Water	Mutable

Table 1

In common usage, a constellation is a group of stars that when connected together form a figure or picture. Some well-known constellations contain striking and familiar patterns of bright stars. Examples are Orion, containing a figure of a hunter, Leo, containing bright stars outlining the form of a lion and Scorpius, a scorpion and so on. The astronomical definition of constellation is slightly different, however. A group of stars that can be connected to form a figure or a picture is called an asterism, while a constellation is an area on the sky. The International Astronomical Union (IAU) divides the sky into 88 official constellations with exact boundaries, so that every direction or place in the sky belongs within one constellation. These are mostly based upon the constellations of the ancient Greek tradition, passed down through the Middle Ages, and contain the signs of the zodiac. The sun appears to pass through the 12 constellations of the zodiac and ancient Greek astronomers believed that they had a special significance. When we look at the constellations of the zodiac, we see that the zodiac signs are either represented by animal figures (Ram for Aries, Bull for Taurus, Crab for Cancer, Lion for Leo, Scorpion for Scorpio, Goat for Capricorn and Fish for Pisces) or by mythological figures (Centaur for Sagittarius) or Twins for Gemini, Woman for Virgo, Man for Aquarius or an object (Scales for Libra). In questioning the meanings of the zodiac signs, or speculating on their choices, does not lead us anywhere near to complete conclusions, since they have been conventionally adapted, accepted and passed on from our ancestors, perhaps from the time astrology was born.

My initial impression was that, either the age-old science of astrology has been passed on to us incomplete for six millenniums, or we have lost some of its foundations down the road in history. When studying the sun sign personalities, one can interpret the traits of the animals and the objects to the personalities of the people born in that particular sun sign and not the other way around. For example, the stubbornness of the bull can be related to the Taurus sun sign people, weighing the pros and cons of any situation can be related to Libra sun sign people, pride of the lion to Leo sun sign people, and stinging scorpion trait to Scorpio sun sign people, and so on. But from the dawn of civilizations, there is no record of why the choices of Ram for Aries sign, and why a bull for Taurus sign, and so on is still unknown.

One can only speculate that the water signs are represented by water creatures like the crab, scorpion and the fish, but rest of the animal choices is still a mystery. Moreover, looking up in the night sky one can trace any animal figures by joining stars randomly. So, what is the significance of this zodiac signs anyway? One can also argue that the stars that make up constellations are so many millions light years away from our solar system and their influence on life on earth or even on human affairs will be insignificant. Even within our solar system, the gravitational influence of the larger planets like Jupiter, Saturn, Uranus or Neptune will be trivial compared to the immense influence of the Sun on planet earth, so how did this science of astrology received so much attention since the beginning of our civilization? One can also wonder how astrology has survived six or even more millenniums until today.

Now, I want to use the analogy of genetics as an example, where Gregory Mendel is consider the father of modern genetic, but he had no clue as to how a DNA molecule looked like when he proposed the theory of inheritance of traits through genes in 19th century, and his work was not recognized until the turn of the 20th century. Also, only recently are we beginning to get a clearer picture of the Darwinian theories of evolution. If

Darwin and Mendel were to be alive today, the volumes of genetic information we have today about most plants and animals, would really amaze them. Anyway, who ever was the pioneer behind the science of astrology, either he had incomplete ideas about the true meanings the zodiac signs or their significance. The other possibility is that perhaps we have lost the foundations for astrology, or the study has been passed on to us incomplete in many ways. Some even believe that aliens brought this science to the earth. As we continue our discussions in this book, we will see that the constellations have nothing to do with the design of the zodiac personalities or any significance to astrology at all. Let's begin our journey to decode this science of astrology in the following chapters.

Theory of complementary pairs

Before we proceed to uncover the masks of the individual zodiac signs, we will ponder over the true meanings of the zodiac signs and decode the complementary zodiac-pairs, which would make our further analysis simple and the theory to be valid. Conventionally, creatures, mythological figures or objects based on the stars that suggest them, represent each of the twelve zodiac signs. Though behind some of the representations is a mythological story, the true meanings of the zodiac signs are still unknown, but have been conventionally adopted, accepted, and used from the time since astrology was born. Similarly, the drawings of the zodiac symbols are thought to have first appeared in the Greek texts, and their history is unknown. Most of the symbols seem to be a kind of shorthand picture, a hieroglyph, of the sign.

As we all know, astrology grew up in the background of belief that earth was the center of the universe, and the same convention is still observed for the construction of any astrological chart. Against these strict conventions of astrology, as far as my knowledge about astrology is concerned, no one has ever questioned the meanings of the zodiac signs and their symbols. Thus, astrology has conventionally remained only as a theoretical system of thought that attempts to show a relationship between human and the celestial bodies. Until recently, Linda Goodman's sun signs is one of the very few books ever to discuss the physical features of each zodiac sun sign. Though Linda's work is more focused towards the psychological makeup of the each sun sign personalities and their relationship with one another, a rough idea about the physical features of each signs are mentioned. Most of the physical features described by Linda are true to a certain extend, but lack conceptual and more detailed explanations. For example, I came to find that the physical features described for Taurus and Leo were the most fitting to the zodiac signs they represent. I completely understand the difficulties that Linda could have faced, in describing the physical features of each sun sign, without a concrete meaning for the zodiac signs, a new factor of complementary zodiac-pairs, and other overlapping factors, which we will see later. Now, we will see the need for redefining the meanings of the zodiac signs and the theory of complementary pairs in the following section, before we proceed to analyze the physical features.

Any hypothesis or theory is based on an allowance of a certain degree of assumptions to be made. Let's begin our analysis from the word zodiac itself, which means circle of animals. We see that the zodiac signs are represented not only by animals, but also by creatures or object (in the case of Libra represented by a balance) and also human mythological figures. Now, when we take a closer look at the zodiac signs by each of the elements they belong to, starting from the fire signs, Aries is represented by a ram, Leo by a lion and Sagittarius by a centaur, half man-half horse figure. We will assume here that Sagittarius as being represented only by a horse to comply with the true meaning of the word zodiac. Next, we move on to the earth signs where Taurus is represented by a bull or cow in my assumptions, Virgo by a woman and Capricorn by a half goat-half fish figure. Here also, we will assume that Capricorn as being represented only by an antelope. Also, Virgo represented by a woman can be related to the female ape or an ape-woman, again to comply with the meaning of the word zodiac.

In the case of air signs, Gemini is represented by a twin human figure, Libra by a balance and Aquarius by a man or ape-man watering the field.

We can try to explain the choice of twins for the zodiac sign Gemini as follows. The main reason, of course, is because of the constellation Gemini, which resembles very close to two human figures holding hands, with the stars Pollux and Castor as their heads, respectively. Based on my speculations, the reason could be because of the double personality of its individuals that is imposed on them by their ruling planet mercury, which has its one side always exposed to the sun and the other always turned away due to the high lineal speed and slow spin around its axis. Also, the other could be for the reason that on an average of 65 days out of the 365 days in a year, the planet mercury is in retrograde, or in apparent backward motion with respect to the earth (i.e., in a cycle of two months forward motion and 20 days in retrograde and so on). Similarly, the choice of scales for Libra is probably due to the justic nature of the zodiac sign and the typical characteristic of considering both sides of a problem before taking any decision. And finally, in case of the water signs, a crab represents Cancer; Scorpio by a scorpion and Pisces is represented by a pair of fishes. We see that all these creatures are from the water, chosen probably, to represent only the water element of the zodiac signs. We could only speculate on the reasons and meanings for the zodiac signs, but we will never know their true intent.

Generally, when we look at the 12 zodiac signs, each represented by different creatures or objects, it doesn't convey any information about the physical features of its native at all nor has been thought of, except by Linda, of course. But, when we scrutinize the blueprint of the zodiac map in the sky, based on an assumption of complementary pairs, we could see an encoded message depicting the pattern of evolution of recent land mammals. Our ancestors, who partially discovered this truth about the heavens, left behind with us astrology, only as a system of thought that connects the human to the celestial bodies. My own personal study, based on speculations and facial observations, led me to uncover some more interesting secrets of the heavens, which we would see as below.

In my quest for answers and after many years of observation and research, I stumbled upon a new theory of complementary pairs in astrology. While observing the physiognomy of the zodiac sun signs, as a part of my hobby to recognize sun signs of people, I came to find that there were many features common between only certain pair of zodiac signs. For example, Aries and Scorpio were stamped with a common feature of penetrating eyes, Taurus and Libra with fleshy upper and lower lips (Note: please do not associate or confuse with the big lips of African American people, which is a genetic trait, something similar to the oriental eyes), Gemini and Capricorn stamped with an ageless facial appearance, and so on. The explanation for this observation can only be given by a new theory of complementary pairs in astrology, which will be discussed in more details below.

Male – Female / Positive - Negative	
Complementary pairs	**Land mammals**
Aries - Scorpio	Ram – Sheep
Taurus – Libra	Bull - Cow
Gemini – Capricorn	Male – Female Antelope
Cancer – Sagittarius	Horse - Mare
Leo – Pisces	Lion - Lioness
Aquarius - Virgo	Male – Female Ape

Table 2

In nature, we see that every male has a complementary female counterpart, except of course for the hermaphrodite earthworms. Now, if we

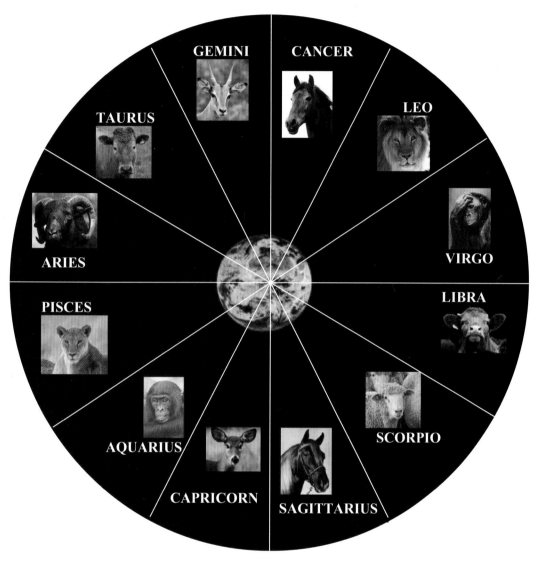

Figure 2

extrapolate the same concept to astrology, the complimentary pair theory can be summarized as in table 2 and as seen in figure 2. As we can see from table 2, there are only six pairs of animals representing the zodiac signs, with six males and their six female counterparts, thus in compliance with the true meaning of the word zodiac. Now, let's revisit the conventional zodiac representations in table 3 below that have been passed on to us since the beginning of astrology. Let's look closer at the first six representations; we see that the zodiac representation follows the similar land mammals in my complementary pair theory except for the twins and the crab. Taurus is a feminine sign, so it cannot be a bull but a cow in my assumptions. The Virgo represented by the virgin is actually assumed in my theory as female ape (again to comply with the word zodiac).

Zodiac signs	Zodiac representations
Aries	Ram
Taurus	Bull
Gemini	Twins
Cancer	Crab
Leo	Lion
Virgo	Virgin woman
Libra	Balance
Scorpio	Scorpion
Sagittarius	Centaur (half man half horse)
Capricorn	Sea goat
Aquarius	Water bearing man
Pisces	Two fishes

Table 3

Now, if we look at the complementary pairs of Gemini and Cancer, which is Capricorn and Sagittarius, Capricorn is represented by a goat, which I want to represent as an antelope in my theory. And, Sagittarius is represented by centaur (which is definitely a Greek influence), but still there is an element of horse in the representation, which is definitely not a coincidence. Similarly, Aquarius is a masculine sign represented by a water bearing man, which is assumed to be a male ape in my complementary theory again to comply with the word zodiac. As one can see, my complementary theory fits very well into my assumptions from the conventional representation of the zodiac signs.

The sequence of the six animals is placed in a correct order, as we see from Aries to Virgo. Later from Libra to Pisces, the animal sequence is slightly changed as depicted in table 3 by the arrows. We see that Libra and Scorpio being interchanged; next Sagittarius and Capricorn being interchanged, and finally Aquarius and Pisces are also interchanged. The interchanges of these zodiac signs are very much in consensus with the following five important zodiac-chart factors. 1) The maintenance of Fire-Earth-Air-Water sequence throughout the entire chart, 2) the trine of elements at every 120 degrees, 3) the alternative arrangement of the positive (male) and negative (female) zodiac signs, 4) the sequence of Cardinal-Fixed-Mutable qualities and 5) the fact that Fire signs always opposed by Air signs and the Earth signs always opposed by a Water sign. To put it in a simple physicist's way of expression, we see that the net astrological energy of the zodiac circle around the earth is zero. Now, it becomes very clear to us that there is some kind of order in the arrangement of the signs in the zodiac map and it is indeed some kind of a coded blueprint. One more point to note here is that, when we take two pairs at a time, for example Aries and Taurus, their energy field is neutralized by Scorpio and Libra on the other side of the zodiac. The same is true for Gemini/Cancer and Leo/Virgo pairs.

The following hypothesis is just to support my theory of complementary pairs in astrology and its connection with the sequence of the evolutionary hierarchy in the most recent mammals. Now, if we take a closer look at the animals in table 2, they represent the most recent land mammals, and almost all the different species of mammals on earth, including humans, fall only into this six different mammal species. The sequence of animals also represents the evolutionary hierarchy with the four herbivorous, hoofed mammals having a common evolutionary path, while the carnivorous lion and the omnivorous ape with a common ancestry.

When we look at the herbivorous mammals, the ram or sheep is the smallest of them all. In the evolutionary step, the bull or cow evolved to become stronger and bigger to defend from predators. In the subsequent evolutionary step, the antelope evolved to be agile and faster to defend from predators. At the top of the herbivorous ladder is the horse, which evolved to be stronger, agile and faster. Now, when we look at the shapes and placement of the ears of the herbivorous mammals, the physical evidence further attest the path of evolution in the above sequence. Again, this is just my logical arguments to support my theory.

The sheep has its ears more close to the ground sensing vibrations on the ground and close range sounds from possible predators. Its ears are set flat to the ground, little below their eyes and sometimes hanging down the sides. Now, if we look at the ears of bull or cow, they are pointed upwards and placed in line with their eyes to hear sounds coming from farther distance from their predators. The antelopes on the other hand have their ears placed above their eyes and further pointed upwards. And in the horse, the ears are placed well above their head possible for rotation in all four directions. Since the book is not about evolution of land mammals, I would like to close this discussion here. At least, we see the evolutionary sequence of the herbivorous mammals and the sequence of the zodiac signs are similar, which is definitely not a coincidence. In my opinion, evolution is not a random event but a gradual represented of a predetermined sequence of events, which is very early to conclude at this point (more discussions in chapter 6).

☼

☼

Astromasks

Having discussed the theory of complementary pairs, we will now analyze the physiognomy of each individual zodiac signs, represented by each of the animals in the series, which I call the "Astromasks". We start from the lowest step in the zodiac ladder, the Aries-Scorpio pair, represented by Ram in the fire element, and Sheep in the water element. Like the Ram and Sheep, Aries and Scorpio are very small built, relatively a hairy body and a gruff voice. The female members of the Aries-Scorpio pair are stamped with big breasts, not in proportion to the size of the whole body, just like the sheep. Both Aries and Scorpio are prone to selfish, impulsive, rash behaviors, and both seek and enjoy revenge. The eyes are piercing with hypnotic intensity and bore deeply into you, as if they're penetrating your very soul. There is a pair of prominent bone structure hanging over on either side of the eyebrows, as shown in the figure. The eyebrows are stubby and meet over the nose forming a bridge. The nose is big and very prominent in the face next to the eyes, with a typical hook shaped, and a typical split ending as seen in the figures. The mouth is small with the upper lips exposing the front teeth and gum, even when the mouth is closed.

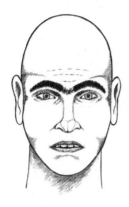

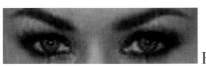 Hypnotic eyes of Aries

 Split nose of Scorpio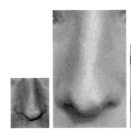

 Aries mouth exposing the teeth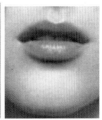

 Henry James (April 15, 1843)

Adolf Hitler (April 20, 1889)

Bette Davis (April 5, 1908)

The next step in the ladder is the Taurus-Libra pair, represented by Cow in the earth element and the Bull in the air element. Like the Bull and the Cow, Libra and Taurus are strong and hefty built, almost a hairless body and a soft, sexy voice. The female members of the Taurus-Libra pair are also stamped with big breasts, like the Cow, but in proportion to the whole body. Both men and women have well-balanced figures. The men are generally handsome and the women very beautiful with a well-proportioned body. Both Taurus and Libra are artistic, sensual, diplomatic, stubborn, with a general aesthetic sense, and prone to a lavish, luxurious life-style. Both Taurus and Libra are pleasure seeking, sometimes lazy and procrastinating, which could lead to over-weight problems. In Taurus and Libra, the eyes are big, clear and very beautiful, as in the bull. The prominent pair of bone structure is now placed right above the eyes right at the eyebrows. The nose is less prominent, but ends with a typical heart-shaped structure similar to the bull. Other details can be seen in the figure. The ears are normally small, with a typical curved structure and placed very close to the head. The mouth is big with strong teeth exposing the gums and with fleshy upper and lower lip.

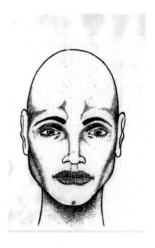

The general bone structure of the face is strong and sturdy with pronounced cheek. The contour of the face is as shown in the figure, with a high forehead, and usually with a lock of hair hanging over a high forehead as in the bull. There is a typical dimple at the lower chin, as seen in the above figures below.

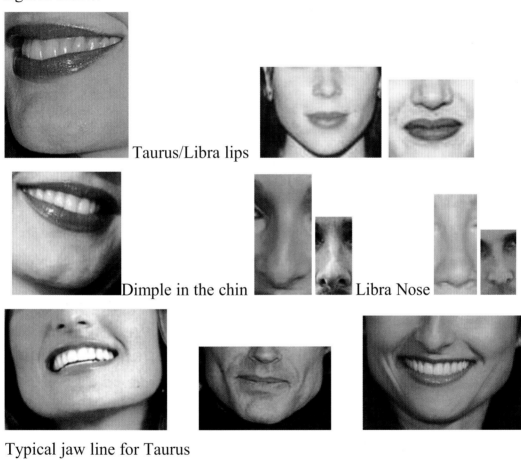

Taurus/Libra lips

Dimple in the chin   Libra Nose

Typical jaw line for Taurus

Audrey Hepburn (May 4, 1929)

Further up the ladder, we see the Gemini-Capricorn pair, represented by the male Antelope in the air element and female Antelope in the earth element. They are strong, lanky built, with good bone structure, a moderately hairy body and quite a gruff voice. Like the antelopes, Gemini and Capricorn are stamped with a classical disappearance act and a blend of deceit. The deceptive nature of the Gemini is not expressed openly in Capricorn people; it is very subtle and can pop up occasionally with a clever excuse. Both are very clever in getting what they want at the expense of others. They are very intelligent, verbal, versatile, dexterous, goal-oriented and cunning in their personal traits. Both are able to manage more than one task at a time. In Gemini and Capricorn, the eyes are beautiful, crystal-clear hazels that dart here and there with a twinkle, and almost pop out. The face gives a young look even at middle age, which is similar to the ageless look on the antelopes. The pair of prominent bone structure seen in the ram and bull now is moved further, closer to the nose, hanging in the inner side of the

eyebrows. The eyebrows meet in the middle, forming a bridge over the nose. The nose is long with a hump in the middle. Both the lower and upper lips are fleshy. The ears form a web structure at bottom and are pronounced on the top. The teeth are beautiful, uniformly arranged and are not so prominent in the mouth as in the antelopes.

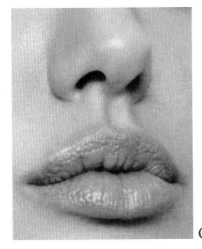
Gemini Lips

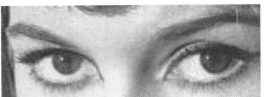

Gemini ears

Gemini eyes

Marilyn Monroe (June 1, 1926)

John F. Kennedy (May 29, 1917)

The Cancer-Sagittarius pair, represented by the mare in the water element and horse in the fire element, occupies fourth step in the ladder. They are the tallest, sturdy built among all the zodiac signs, with a large skull and strong bone structure, a moderately hairy body, and a shrill tone of voice. The men usually become bold with age. Female members of both Cancer and Sagittarius are stamped with very small breasts, not in proportion to the size of the body, just like the mare. Cancer and Sagittarius adore dangerous sports, the Cancer people in the water and the Sagittarians in racing and fire sports. Both, posses a typical loud horselaugh that runs up and down the scales with a deep, throaty undertone. Both will be the center of attention, funny and quite noisy people in a party. In Cancer and Sagittarius, the eyes are deeply set with an overhanging brow. The skull is fairly large with a pronounced lower jaw and high cheekbones.

The pair of prominent bone structure is now placed right above the eyebrows on either side resulting in the deeply set appearance of the eyes. The eyes are the most widely set in the face compared to the other zodiac masks similar to the horse. The ears are placed facing the front at the bottom, with a prominent protruding ear-lobe piece at the bottom, as shown in the figure.

The mouth is wide open showing the prominent big teeth and gum, which are placed slanting outwards as in the horse. The tongue is usually small in relation to the size of the mouth, rounded and placed inside the mouth similar to the horse. The nose is overhanging and very prominent in the face. The lower jaw moves in similar trend as in the horse with a prominent slant. Just below the lower lip, there is a pair of bulged features similar to that in the horse.

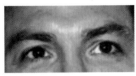 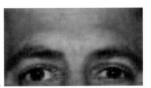

Cancer /Sagittarius forehead

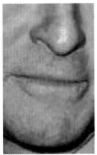 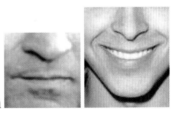

Cancer nose and mouth

Princess Diana (July 1, 1961)

Up next, in the cycle is the Leo-Pisces pair represented by the carnivorous beast Lion in the fire element and the Lioness in the water element. Leo and Pisces are lanky built, with a curved in stomach, and rough voice almost coming from the nose. Both sexes have a moderately hairy body. Female members of both Leo and Pisces are stamped with the largest breast area compared to any other zodiac signs. Leo and Pisces are loners at soul, with a sympathetic heart, and violent behaviors from time to time; the Leo can be aggressive, the Piscean nagging and sarcastic. Both are attracted to the arts, theater, and music, and wherever there is a need for expression of the self. They both are very much sports oriented and love to teach, thus end up as educators. In Leo and Pisces, the eyes are small and placed slightly slanting in the inner side near the nose. The forehead shows wrinkled creasing lines. The pair of prominent bone structure is now placed in the middle of the forehead, visible as in the case of lion and in the other cats. The eyebrows are stubby at the end. The hump on the nose is placed right at the top of the nose very close to the forehead. The mouth is noticeably slanting, exposing the lower jaw teeth, with prominent canine teeth, and with a fleshy lower lip as in the lion. The upper part of the mouth is prominent and extended as in the lion.

The lower lip is fleshier than the upper lip. The teeth from both jaws are irregular and locked when speaking. The ears are protruding upwards as in all the cats. The space between the nose and mouth is little stretched and shows a movement similar to the cats. There are prominent dimples on either side of the cheeks. The lower chin is little protruding and split by a groove. There are three prominent ridges just below the lower lip.

Leo slanting eyes and cheek bones

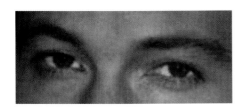
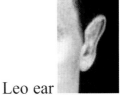

Leo ear

George Bernard Shaw (July 26, 1856)

The final step in the series is the Virgo-Aquarius pair represented by the female Ape in the earth element and male Ape in the air element. Both Virgo and Aquarius are quite strongly built, with a well-shaped skull, a more hairy body and a normal tone of voice. The legs look shorter than their hands in the general body proportion and there is a typical waddle or limp in their walking posture. Both Virgo and Aquarius are humanitarians with service-oriented minds, prone to worry and becoming restless. Both can appear like an absent-minded professor with serious thoughts in their minds, talking unnecessarily and completely forgetting their main purpose. They are very curious learners and are born geniuses. Their verbal dexterity makes them excellent political speakers, leaders who will fight for the causes of the masses. In Virgo and Aquarius, the eyes are very beautiful, clear, with a vague, dreamy, wandering expression and sparkle with intelligence. The eyes are placed the closest to each other compared to other zodiac masks.

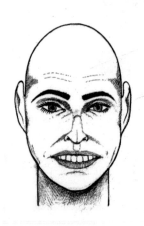

In general, the face gives an impression that there's a serious problem in the mind they are struggling to solve, or a vague feeling that they are secretly worried about something. The nose is very prominent in the face with a dip at the top similar to the ape. The ears are typically small at the bottom and wide at the top and placed close to the head. The pair of prominent bone structure is now very small, placed just above the nose and almost not visible. The lower lip is typically protruding and hanging out very similar to in the ape. The upper-jaw teeth are placed pressing the lower lips. The teeth are irregular and very prominent in the mouth. The nose is overhanging with a split end.

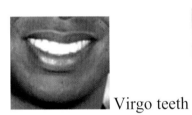 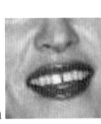 

Virgo teeth

Virgo nose

Abraham Lincoln (February 12, 1809)

Astropersonality

From my experience and observations, only the six inner celestial bodies are responsible for the design of our astropersonality, while the outer planets decide our life path and our future generations in the long run. Moreover, the physiognomy of an individual is an overlapping of the Sun sign, Ascendant sign (Earth sign), Moon sign, Mercury sign, Mars sign, and Venus sign, respectively. Though the most obviously seen physical trait are only the Sun sign, the Ascendant and the Moon sign, simply for the reasons that these three are the most close celestial bodies, which have the strongest influence on anything on earth. The Ascendant sign is defined as the rising sign on the horizon from the place an event is occurring. The following illustration will explain how ascendant sign is simply the position of earth in the celestial sphere from the place of birth. Imagine a person who is born at the point where the latitude and the longitude (represented by the dotted lines) meet as indicated by the figure, his/her ascendant sign is on the horizon, which is exactly on the opposite side of the earth.

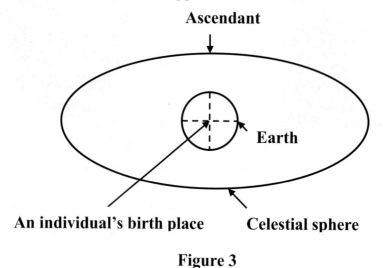

Figure 3

Relative to the place of his/her birth or where the event is occurring on the surface of earth, the ascendant sign is the placement of earth on the celestial sphere. So, no matter where the person is born on earth his/her ascendant sign will be the placement of earth on the zodiac circle relative to the place of birth. The positions of the planets at the precise moment of our birth, the date, time and place, represents our natal horoscope. As most of us know, the sun sign personifies the soul or one's own higher self within (our character), the ascendant or earth sign reveals the person as others see us (our personality), the moon sign conveys our emotional needs (our sentiments), the placement of mercury tells us the way we think and communicate (our intellect), the placement of Venus reveals our expression of love and affection (our romantic nature) and the placement of Mars shows our general drives in life, our expression power and our goals in life (our cardinal character).

Ever since we take our first breath on this earth, we are stamped with the unique characteristic personality and a life cycle, depending on the placement of the planets in our natal chart. As the title of this book tells you, here we will concentrate only on the characteristic features seen on the face of a person, their significance and relation to his or her sun sign, earth sign and moon sign, respectively. Let me illustrate with the following horoscope in figure 5. We see that the person is born with the Sun in Virgo, Moon in Taurus, Ascendant or Earth in Aries, Mercury in Cancer, Mars in Gemini and Venus in Leo. So, the person born with this horoscope is stamped with the astromask of female ape (Sun), Ram (Earth), Cow (Moon), Horse (Mercury), male Antelope (Mars) and Lion (Venus). Now, as I mentioned earlier, only the sun sign, moon sign and the earth sign design our physiognomy, with the most obvious visible facial features being our ascendant or earth sign.

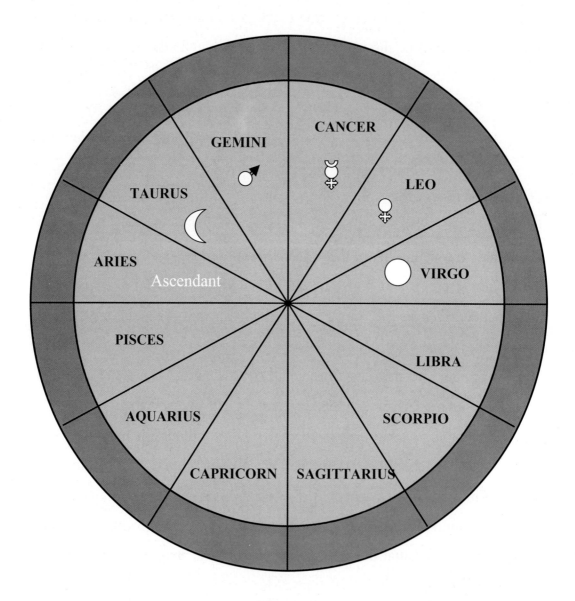

Figure 4

Cosmic conclusions

We all know that humans have 99% common DNA molecules with all the six land mammals listed in table 2, which means that we already have the genes to design our physiognomy similar to the animals that make the complementary pairs. So, when the egg meets with the sperm and implants itself in the uterus, the horoscope of that individual is predetermined from the position of the planets at the precise moment of the fertilization day, time and place (I would like to call this as the fertilization horoscope). So, as we grow in the mother's womb, our physiognomy is pre-designed to be born only on a particular date, time and place. The correlation between the fertilization horoscope and the birth horoscope of an individual is still under research. I have already established a clear correlation between the parent's horoscope and their offspring's horoscope, which will be published in my future book, "Astrogenes". As mentioned above, the physiognomy of an individual is an overlapping of the Sun sign, the Ascendant and the Moon sign, which are the most obviously seen physical traits in a face. When we leave the mother's womb and take the first breath on earth, we are stamped with the astromasks corresponding to the position of the planets at the time of our birth. How does astrology affect our life path? The energy field produced around the earth, by the placement of the planets at a particular time in our life, relative to our natal horoscope, decides the choices we make in life, and thus affecting our life journey.

Another important conclusion to be made here is that the zodiac signs represented in the constellations have nothing to do with the design of our astromasks. My speculation is that the energy field changes around the earth, relative to the placement of the sun and planets around the earth in the zodiac signs is responsible for directing the genetic materials, in the fertilized egg, to design the human with a particular physiognomy and hence his/her horoscope. My speculations tempt me to conclude further that, even the evolution of animals is a recorded message happening in a sequence in a large span of time-sale. Stretching the theory even further, I would say that the whole universe is a living entity, though in a different dimension of time-scale.

Physicists and astronomers may believe in the Big Bang theory of the universe and life molecules being brought into earth from outer space, (making us think that the life molecules for making a chicken come from outside the egg shell). But when we look close at nature, all things are made to live and die. Even the stars have a life cycle of birth and death, just like a living cell, though in a different dimension of time-scale. Also, we see that there is a systematic evolution of elements in the periodic table from hydrogen. When from a single cell, the whole animal or human body is generated, with the help of the coded message in the DNA; can we not extrapolate the same idea to the birth of universe, the galaxies and the stars. Logically, our body is also created in a similar big bang way, growing in size from a single cell, until we become old and die. This same pattern is also seen in all the plants and other animals. And, when we look deep into our bodies, in the atomic scale, we are just made of a regular arrangement of atoms, but as a whole, we are living. For example, let us consider the following analogy of a human being, in the size of a protein molecule, standing on the surface of the Mitochondria inside a living cell, observing the neighboring cells and trying to imagine the vastness of the whole organ, or the whole living animal, of which it is just a fractional part. The human protein molecule will observe all the nuclei as millions and millions of stars, in the similar way we humans observe the nuclei of the other solar systems as stars and the other organs as galaxies. Similarly, everything in this universe is living, though in different dimensions.

Moreover, if we consider random mutations and natural selection as the only reasons for evolution, looking at the perfect designs of nature's creations, there is nothing that is random. Also, the random mutations could only lead to non-uniform, life forms, something like the creatures we see in sci-fi movies. But we see that, all land animals have perfect design features, which are only possible from a predetermined sequence of events for evolution. With evolution, we see that there is a uniform addition of genetic materials, and a gradual, uniform change in the physical forms of the animals. All events on earth seem to be occurring in a kind of sequence, which could only be explained by a theory of preplanned and pre-stored information in the heavens. I would like to call this as the conscious cosmic evolution.

And, why did not the evolution continue beyond human? As per my speculations, the energy field around the earth at this era of life cycle on earth has a predetermined final step of human as the most evolved creature on earth. Only astrology can provide the answers and explanations for all these questions. The material for such a discussion would be enough for another book, at a latter point in time.

☼

After word

Here I am, a complete self-made atheist,
Hoping my best to give you a spiritual feast.
Believe me; I am trying to act like a priest,
But tell you some truth, all from my spiritual quest.

Human beings have long lived on planet earth,
Hoping one day, god will tell them the truth.
Because, never did they realize that god is just a myth.
But, what is the role of so called god in this earth?

Have you ever asked this or given it a thought?
Hoping, we are all here to pass the god-given test.
But, why all this? Is god a hardcore sadist?
But no, because there is no god nor did he exist.

How many problems just in the name of gods?
Hundreds of wars to prove the best among lords.
But, Is there an end to all this or could we avoid?
Believe me, if only we could think and act with words.

How many religions and sects are yet to be born?
Hundreds of week-mind, so easily drawn, only to be torn.
Because, never did even science reveal the entire religious con,
But also, the sixth-sense is yet to be cloned for many in our clan.

Hopes of peace fast diminishing in our ever-fragile Eden,
Humans, if only realize soon, earth is our only heaven.
Because, happiness and sadness are both made here within.
But, the choice is up to us, either heaven or let pain to win.

Let's move on from here to explore this age-old concept.
Let me call it, "Universal Religion of Astrology", lest we forget.
Lots of saints have told us in the past, which I'll not repeat.
Let's leave the past behind to enter this new sphere of thought.

Repeating exactly in Linda's words, "I've shared my personal discoveries of truth with you because I believe that any kind of search implies an obligation to exchange with others what has been found, in the interest of hastening the sunrise of harmony on earth, the ultimate peace". I trust that my findings would make way for other astrologers and scientists to decipher the remaining secrets of the heaven and the true meanings of our universe. The seeds of wisdom are contained in all scriptures ever written, especially in art, music, poetry, and above all, in nature. Nature and astrology are synonymous in many ways, conveying the same sense and meaning to the life on this exclusive planet of ours called Earth. Astrology extends the meaning of life out into the space, to the celestial bodies and to the universe as a whole. Thousands of questions can be asked to find answers to the meaning of life on earth. The answers are all up there, coded in the heavens, to be revealed at the right moment and at the right celestial configurations. Astrology is the only answer to all good and bad, to all happiness and suffering, and to all birth and death in this universe.

Another interesting fact, which I have observed, is a regular pattern in the placement of the planets in the offspring's natal chart, in relation to the father's and the mother's natal charts. In most instances, the offspring has the facial features, either close to that of the dad or to that of the mom. Now, if this could be related only to the reason, because of the genetic connections, there should be some explanation for the correlations that I have seen between the parent's and the offspring's natal charts. Or, the placement of the planets in a natal chart is in some way connected to the genetic material of the human? Also, many astrologers would agree with me that the placement of planets in a natal chart is an indicator for several diseases, but most of the chronic diseases are genetic in origin. What is the connection between the genetics and the celestial bodies? Answers to all these questions will form the main theme of my next research book, ''Astrogenes'', after I have seen the comments and critics for my new theory of complementary pairs in astrology. Let me just give some time for everyone to view astrology in this new light.

Finally, I thank you all for joining me in this first phase of the long journey, in the world of astrology and in the quest for the truth. For truth only can set us all free.

Mars - ruler of complementary pairs Aries-Scorpio

About the book

Astromasks is the first book of its kind. By introducing the new theory of complementary pairs in astrology for the very first time ever, it probes the fundamental basics of astrology, the true meanings of the zodiac signs, and their connection to human on earth, which has never been done before in the entire history of astrology. It supports the theory with physical evidences observed on individuals. Complementary pair theory also adds a new dimension to astrology, thus giving a whole new perspective of astrology, and takes astrology to an even higher level of accepting it as a true science. The theory also compares astrology with the theory of evolution, and thus speculates on a new meaning to the life on earth, which occurs in a sequence of events dictated by the conscious evolution. Digging even further into the core of astrology, the book discusses the predetermined birth of an individual from the moment of his/her conception in the womb. The book tries its best to give complete meaning to the age-old science of astrology, which has been passed on to us incomplete in many ways for over six millenniums, and adds to the possible lost features. Personally, I strongly feel that the theory of complementary pairs is the final answer to all the questions ever raised by anyone skeptic about the authenticity of this amazing and intriguing science, during the entire history of astrology.

As addressed above, Astromasks is unique in many ways and can be of interest to general audience in helping them recognize sun sign personalities based on physical, mental and emotional characters, and also relationship issues. Giving a new meaning to the zodiac signs, without much altering the other basic foundations of astrology, such as sequence of elements, arrangement of the cardinal, fixed and mutable signs, trine of elements at 120 degrees and more, this book would be useful to classical astrologers in better understanding their clients. The book gives a new meaning to life on earth, which could be of much interest to philosophers and scientists alike.

Venus - ruler of complementary pairs Libra-Taurus

Recommended Books and Websites

1. Linda Goodman's Sun Signs.
2. Venus Trines at Midnight by Linda Goodman.
3. Linda Goodman's Love Signs.
4. Linda Goodman's Love Poems.
5. Linda Goodman's Star Signs.
6. Gooberz by Linda Goodman.
7. Linda Goodman's Relationship Signs.

1. http://www.consciousevolution.com/
2. http://www.lovestarz.com/maryalice.html
3. http://www.linda-goodman.com/
4. http://www.solsticepoint.com/astrologersmemorial/goodman.html
5. http://www.astro.com/
6. http://www.astrologyzone.com/
7. http://www.astrologers.com/
8. http://www.aas.org/
9. http://www.astrologicalassociation.com/
10. http://www.mountainastrologer.com
11. http://www.uacastrology.com/
12. http://www.dellhoroscope.com/
13. http://www.astrology.com/
14. http://en.wikipedia.org/wiki/Astrology